A Kid's Guide to Paul Revere

Who Was He and What *Really* Happened on the Midnight Run?

Kids Press

www.eKidsPress.com

An Imprint of Minute Help, Inc.

Table of Contents

About eKids

Adults! Turn away! This book is not for you!

eKids Books is proud to present a new series of books for all the readers who matter the most: Kids, of course!

*"Paul Revere's Ride" in the
National Archives and Records
Administration - identifier
#535721*

Introduction

America in the year 1735 was VERY different from the America of today. There was no electricity for one thing, and there were not many roads either! If you wanted to go visit a friend it might take you a few days to get there because people could only walk or ride a horse - if you had one!

Just think, in 1735, the United States did not exist yet...it was still the 13 original colonies that were ruled by the King back in England. The Colonies were all the way across the Atlantic Ocean, and were home to around 275,000 people who were just starting to build what would one day become the United States.

It was a time when people had trades such as sailing, weaving, cobbling (making shoes), and even teaching. Kids would not usually enjoy a lot of playtime, and would instead begin to work with a skilled person in order to learn a trade.

For instance, young boys would work in the different trades of their fathers, uncles or older brothers. Girls were expected to learn how to manage a home, which was pretty hard work when you realize that they had to do everything from washing clothes to baking bread without any machines, running water, or electricity!

Paul Revere would learn his father's trade of silversmith, but he would become famous for a lot more than the work he did each day! Let's find out more about him and the world that he knew...

Map of Boston from "Boston" by Henry Cabot Lodge written in 1892. Map courtesy of http://openlibrary.org/books/OL 24340247M/Boston

Chapter 1: Paul Revere as a Child and Teen

Paul Revere was born in 1735, in the largest city in the country at that time - Boston, Massachusetts. Though it was thought to be enormous, there were still only around 7,000 people living in the city. (If you can believe it, New York City was SECOND in size with around 5,000 people, and Philadelphia was a very close third.)

By the 1730s, however, there were already some signs that many people living in the Colonies (both in the cities and the towns) were ready to become free of British Rule. This means that around the same time that Paul Revere was born, there were already unwanted taxes being demanded, and people were starting to protest.

This is the world that Paul Revere would grow up in, and it is a good explanation for the famous person he would soon become. Before we learn all about the Revolutionary War, however, let's look at Paul Revere's years as a child and a teenage boy. His early years at home are just as important as the bigger events going on all around him, because they also played a small part in making him so unique and memorable.

His Family and Trade

We know that he was the third of the twelve children that his parents would have, and that he worked in the same trade as his father - as a silversmith. His father was also named Paul Revere (it is interesting to note that his father's real name was Apollos Rivoire, but he changed it when he came to Boston from France at the age of 13).

Being the son of a busy silversmith meant that young Paul grew up watching his father making many different items from the metal known as silver. Back then it was not unusual for people to have many dishes, bowls, platters, forks, knives, spoons, and other household items made from silver, gold or pewter. Many of the professional trades needed the work of silversmiths as well. For example, dentists or doctors would come to the silversmith shop to order many of their tools.

So, Paul Revere began to learn this craft from his father during the earliest years of his life. By the age of 13 he was no longer going to school, but employed as a full time apprentice in his father's workshop. What is so interesting is that the work that Paul Revere did would allow him to meet a lot of different types of people all around Boston. This would become very important many years later when the Revolutionary War began to occur.

Because he was at work by such an early age, he also developed excellent skills. Unlike other silver or goldsmiths, Paul Revere would be paid to make the items AND to decorate them. This means that he was very well known long before the war years arrived.

His Religion

Another interesting thing about Paul Revere during his early years was his habit of questioning and challenging things. This too was useful during the Revolutionary War, but it also caused some fighting between himself and his father. For instance, his father had been what is known as a "Huguenot".

A Hugeunot was someone who was part of the Protestant Reformed Church of France, and who belonged to a group that faced many challenges due to their religious choices. Most of the Hugeunots ended up leaving home to avoid persecution for their beliefs.

Just like the Pilgrims of the 1600s, the Huguenots headed to the Colonies to enjoy religious freedom. Because of this, however, Paul Revere and his father got into some very big arguments during his teenage years. Young Paul had always participated in Puritan religious services with his father, but in his teens he befriended a man who was part of the Church of England.

The Puritans were also a religious group and part of the Protestant religious movement. They were treated badly in England and Europe, and it was not unusual for Huguenots to join Puritan churches in the Colonies.

Because this was part of the same church that had forced his father to head to the United States, however, Paul's participation caused trouble. The father and son would argue about the younger Paul's choices. Because Paul was obedient and reasonable he stopped attending the Church of England services and returned to worship with his father in the Puritan church. This shows that, even at a very young age, Paul was willing to stand up for something that he really believed in, and to also use logic and make good choices.

Becoming an Adult

Sadly, his father died when Paul was 19, and this meant many things for the family and for Paul. The major thing was that he was too young to take control of the family business.

It is not well known if he was struggling for money after his father died, but what is known is that he left Boston to enlist in the provincial army and to fight in the French and Indian War. This means that he was fighting for Great Britain against the French forces on the continent. (The French and Indian War was actually only a part of what is known as the "Seven Years' War" that occurred in many parts of the world.)

Some experts think that Paul Revere participated in the war because it paid better than the silversmith work he was doing, but some also believe that he was simply fighting for his country in the same way that fellow soldiers did. For example, George Washington was a soldier in the French and Indian War, too! Paul Revere did well as a soldier and became a Second Lieutenant during his service.

When he returned home to Boston he was old enough to run the family silversmith shop, and to even name the business after himself! He also decided to get married around the age of 22. In 1757 he married Sarah Orne, and the two settled into married life in Boston.

A famous portrait of Paul Revere painted around 1770 by John Singleton Copley. This is now located at the Museum of Fine Arts in Boston, MA.

Chapter 2: Paul Revere as an Adult

By the age of 22, Paul Revere was married and had the first of his 16 children. (His first wife, Sarah died in 1773 and Paul remarried another woman named Rachel Walker. Both of his wives had 8 children with him!)

He was also earning a reputation as one of the best silversmiths in the city. His skills were so great that he was often hired as an engraver, too. This meant that he would make the object, such as a platter, and then also do all of the decorative carving in the silver.

His business was such a success that he could offer financial support to his sister (who never married) and to his widowed mother as well. Today, historical documents show that thousands of items came out of Paul Revere's silver shop and that they included both large and small items, ranging from plaques and signs to rings and beads.

Remember that Revere's work and professional life allowed him to know many of Boston's citizens and most important residents. As his business became more and more successful, he also continued to build his friendships in the community. Around 1760 he was asked to become one of the founding members of a special group in the city as well.

This group was the Masonic Lodge. This is an organization that still exists today and which likes to do a lot of charitable work in their local communities. They also believe that friendship between people is very important, too, and they meet at special lodges to discuss various issues together.

So, Paul Revere was asked to join in and help to start a new lodge in the growing city of Boston. Along with him were some friends from his days in the French and Indian War, but there were also men from many other parts of Boston society. This is a very important thing because it was first a place where they simply met to discuss business and life in the city, but it soon became a secret place where men of Boston would start to discuss ways to fight Britain and its control over the Colonies.

What control did Britain have over the Colonies? You have to understand that colonies have existed in many different places and in many different ways, but the one thing that makes them all very alike is that they are all part of the "home land".

Living in the Colonies

If you use a dictionary to look up the word "colony" you would see that it is explained as a territory or a region that is under the political control of a state. In the American Colonies there were 13 different places that were all ruled by Britain. This meant that the money, business, and legal rules of England were also followed in places like Connecticut, Massachusetts and Georgia.

Why would that be a problem for the people in Boston? Why would they start to meet in private to complain and seek for ways to escape British rule?

Remember when we discussed the French and Indian War? We learned that it was a small part of a much bigger war known as the Seven Years' War. This was mostly a war between England and France, but it involved a lot of different places and people. It also cost a lot of money to fight the war.

Whenever a government has to pay for something such as a war, it has to also find a way to get money back. Right after the end of the Seven Years' War, the economy in England was very bad. It was in what is known as a "recession". A recession is not unusual after a war, but it meant that people in England had no money to spend, and that there were also no jobs or work available. This led to many businesses being closed forever or for some businesses to come very close to failing.

Because the Colonies were part of the British economy, they also had a recession. This was a very difficult thing to deal with because it meant that very few businesses could continue to grow and prosper.

Chapter 3: The Explanation

The British decided to recover the money that they spent on the Seven Years' War by imposing new taxes on their American colonists. The first was the Stamp Act of 1765. This was an impossible tax because it meant that almost all printed materials in the Colonies had to be made on special paper that had been "stamped" by the official houses back in London.

The colonists didn't have all of the printed materials that we have today. Books, letters, legal documents, magazines and newspapers were all quite rare and valuable. Though more than half of the people in the Colonies could read, the documents that were taxed were not just books for pleasure. No, the Stamp Act tax was applied to almost everything that had printing. This meant that if you had to file a legal document you had to also pay the special new tax on the paper.

The British government was using the tax to pay for the war. They said that it was the colonists who needed them to fight and send troops and so it was the colonists who should pay. This angered the colonists and inspired them to send people of their own over to England to argue with the government (also known as Parliament) that this was not fair.

Paul Revere's Reaction

It also inspired Paul Revere to begin joining in on any resistance to the taxes. Unfortunately, he was also trying to keep his business open but all of the money problems in the Colonies had had an effect on his work. (To try to make more money he even learned how to do some dentistry as a second line of work!)

Even as things got worse for Revere's business he continued to look for ways to help fight the unfair British taxation. He joined the famous "Sons of Liberty" and the stage was set for the beginning of the American Revolutionary War.

Painting of the "Surrender at Yorktown" by John Trumbull

Chapter 4: What was the American Revolution all about?

When Paul Revere was born in 1735 there were around 275,000 people in the Colonies. By 1776, there were around two and a half million people! It had been such a long time since the Colonies were started that very few people living in the Colonies felt like the "British subjects" that they actually were.

Things were not simple, however, because the Colonies really did have to rely on Britain for a lot of things. For example, there were many businesses that had to depend on Britain for all of their trade. The protection of the towns and cities was important, too, and it was managed by British soldiers using British weapons.

The problem was the taxation and the laws. A lot of people who had built up their own personal wealth (such as George Washington and John Hancock) did not like that Britain could take money from them as taxes and could stop them from doing business by making certain rules against them.

This was unfair, and things were even more complicated when the issue of "taxation without representation" was first mentioned.

Taxation Without Representation

Just think of what people like Paul Revere must have felt when they had to pay more and more taxes to the British government and yet they did not have a "voice" over in England. What does that mean? Well, the Stamp Act of 1765 was created in England, but no one from the Colonies was in Parliament to discuss the issue. This meant that the people in the Colonies were not being given the same rights that other Englishmen received.

They were being taxed and it was without their consent or agreement. This was the main reason that representatives were sent to Parliament, but also the reason behind the groups of protestors that gathered together to show that they were very unhappy about this issue.

The first stages of the American Revolutionary War can be seen in the different assemblies, petitions, and organized group protests that resulted from news of the Stamp Act tax. There was even an official "Congress" in New York that gathered to discuss ways of fighting the tax. The protests were often violent and many of the people in charge of collecting the tax were so scared that they quit the job and refused to ask for the money.

Paul Revere's reaction was to join in on the creation of the Sons of Liberty and to begin making engravings that helped to spread the word about the unpleasantness of the British government's treatment of the colonists. That was in 1765, and only three years later the first British troops began arriving in Boston. By 1770, five years after he began working with the Sons of Liberty, the famous Boston Massacre occurred.

The Boston Massacre

By March of 1770 the British government had gotten so worried about the Colonies and the way that residents were fighting the taxation issue that they had many soldiers in the Colonies, and particularly in Boston. They were there, they said, to protect the people in charge of collecting taxes and making sure that British laws were upheld. On March 5th, however, a large and angry crowd began to bother a group of British troops. No one knows why the troops fired their guns into the crowd of colonists, but they did, and they killed three people instantly. Two more died after the event.

Although the soldiers had to go to court over the incident, and were defended by future President John Adams, it did not calm things down in the least. The soldiers left the city and a lot of papers and pictures were made of the event - including a famous engraving by Paul Revere's workshop.

"The Boston Massacre". A popular engraving that is claimed to be the work of Paul Revere.

Though a lot of people say that the Boston Massacre was the next thing to bring about the Revolutionary War, it certainly wasn't the last thing to happen before the war began. For instance, the British would pass a few more acts by the time the first shots were fired in Lexington, Massachusetts.

The Acts That Caused Trouble

We have looked at the Stamp Act and the problems that it caused, but there were also:

- The Townsend Act: this was done in 1767 and was an all new tax put on glass, tea, paper, paint and many other necessary goods shipped from Britain to the colonies. Again, the reasons given for the taxes were to raise the money necessary to pay for the "defense" of the colonies. This meant paying the soldiers, but also the governors, judges and other officials. Naturally, this was unfair because they were still being taxed without having any representation in Parliament.

Additionally, there was some trouble because the taxes were being used to provide pay salaries for people who were making sure that British rule was the only rule - and this was not a popular thing to do. Protests were so big that all of the taxes were cut except those on tea. This provided the Colonies with two years of peace and quiet, but then things began to get tense again;

- The Tea Act: this is not a tax act but it is something that happened because of taxes. Although the British Parliament ended the Townsend Act and left only the tax on tea, the residents of the Colonies were still very angry. For one thing, they could only get tea from the companies that Britain allowed. So, people stopped buying tea from approved merchants and started buying it secretly from sources in the country of Holland.

Once again, Britain interfered and created the Tea Act of 1773. This allowed the one British tea company (the British East India Company) to sell to the colonists at a cost even lower than the tea from Holland, even with the added tax. This meant that the colonists had no choices at all and HAD to pay the tax. This led to people once again saying that they had "taxation without representation".

This is what led to the famous "Boston Tea Party": It was in 1773 that the Sons of Liberty decided to head to Boston Harbor and protested the entire Tea Tax issue by throwing three full boat loads of tea into the harbor. This was more than ninety thousand pounds of tea!

- The Intolerable Acts: the Boston Tea Party only made British authorities even more determined. They made four new laws, but the colonists in Boston called them only the "intolerable acts". They were:

  o Boston Harbor was closed until the people of the city paid for all of the ruined tea - with all of the taxes added to the price.

o The ending of the elected
government council of
Massachusetts residents. Instead
the council would be filled with
people chosen by the King of
England. Governors would now
have new authority that allowed
them to control all public meetings
and gatherings, and the Justice Act
was changed so that anyone who
was to go to trial for a violent
crime would have to be sent to
England to face the courts.

o The Quartering Act was expanded.
This was considered the worst of
all because it allowed for British
soldiers to be housed in a person's
private home. This meant that
citizens would have no choice if
the soldier had to sleep, eat and
stay in their home.

o The Quebec Act was passed which
gave Canada all of the land south
to the Ohio River. This meant that
the colonies had much less land
available than ever before, and this

meant that the colonies were going to remain small and controllable.

What Happened After That?

By now you can probably see how people might react to such horrible treatment, but the British Parliament failed to see that something bad might happen when they made these laws. They thought that they could "make an example" of the people of Massachusetts, but instead they upset all of the other colonies and inspired most of them to act out against Britain together.

By 1774, all of the colonial leaders had decided to have their very first "Congress". All thirteen colonies would send representatives to determine how they should react to the new laws, the "Intolerable Acts" that had been put upon the people of Massachusetts.

The First Continental Congress

They came together in Philadelphia (except the representatives from Georgia, who where were blocked by their own governor from attending). They didn't consider independence at this time, but instead wanted to:

1. State their rights

2. Point out that the Parliament was violating their rights

3. Create a plan to get their rights returned

To force things to happen, they also decided to boycott (refuse to buy) any British goods. They also all agreed to meet again in 1775 if nothing happened after they sent their declarations to Britain.

Instead of getting recognized as citizens, the British government decided to punish the Colonies and blocked all access to North Atlantic fishing grounds.

Lexington and Concord

The "shot heard round the world" was fired in Lexington, Massachusetts in April of 1775. It was when the British sent a few hundred soldiers to destroy ammunition and guns in the hands of colonists in the town of Concord, Massachusetts. There were also orders to arrest several leaders in the "patriot movement".

This was Paul Revere's shining moment in history. As a member of the Sons of Liberty and a truly dedicated patriot to the colonial cause, he had remained in Boston and continued to meet often with his fellow Freemasons. They were busy watching and monitoring all of the British soldiers in the area. In December of 1774 he enjoyed his first "ride" to warn the town of Portsmouth, New Hampshire of the arrival of British troops. It was in the following year, however, that his most famous ride occurred.

Understanding the Revolution

Not long after Revere's famous ride, the colonists had to declare themselves independent from Britain. Because the American continent was abundant with so many resources, the British would not just let the colonists leave. They tried to force them back into control by waging war against them. It took many years, but by 1783, the Treaty of Paris had been signed and the United States was free of unfair taxation, unfair treatment, and no longer had a King but a President instead!

There were many things that caused the war, but we now understand that it was taxes and a lot of horrible treatment that forced the colonists to fight for liberty. They started with small steps, but by the night of Paul Revere's ride, most were ready to declare themselves free men and women and to begin fighting for their new country.

Chapter 5: The "Midnight Ride"

"Listen my children and you shall hear
Of the midnight ride of Paul Revere..."

by Henry Wadsworth Longfellow

So, is the poem true or a legend? Did he really ride to spread the alarm? Did he slip past British war ships? Did he warn the countryside? As a matter of fact, he did!

Here's what happened: One of the Sons of Liberty, Dr. Joseph Warren, learned that the British planned to head to Lexington to make arrests and to Concord to destroy ammunition and guns. He informed Paul Revere, who had already been serving as a rider and who was sounding any alarms possible when British soldiers were on the move.

Because there were so few roads in and out of the city, however, Revere was never sure if he would be able to dash out of town and deliver any messages. So, he came up with a great plan: he would use lanterns to send messages if he was stuck in the city. What he did was brilliant - he had told the sexton of North Church (a man named Robert Newman) to use the lanterns in the church tower to inform the colonists of the movement of all of the troops.

Today we hear that the signals were "one if by land and two if by sea". That night he asked Dawson to signal to the town of Charlestown that the troops were headed there by a land route. He then took the daring task of crossing the Charles River in a rowboat. This was totally forbidden and he would have been killed if captured. He made it across and then began the ride to Lexington.

Because of the choice to warn Charlestown ahead of time, the message was spread in all directions by many other riders. There are estimates that more than 30 other people were warning of the coming soldiers thanks to Revere's plans and signal.

The story does not end there because many don't realize that Revere managed the ride even though British patrols were on the same road. So, the only legend we have to say is not true is the one that says he rode through the night shouting: "The British are coming!" He would have certainly been captured had he done that. Instead, he spoke to those he encountered and simply stated: "the Regulars are coming out" which was code for "the British are coming!"

He was able to reach Lexington around midnight and then headed on to Concord. It was on his way there that he was actually captured by the British. They held him at gunpoint, even though he warned them that they were in danger because of the large group of patriots waiting in Lexington. The troops ignored Revere's warning and kept marching towards the town.

Half of a mile from Lexington the very first shot was fired. The British major in charge asked Revere what this shot meant, and he said that it was a warning signal that was meant to alert all of the countryside that the British soldiers had arrived. He also let them know that it meant that they were surely going to die because the militiamen were armed and waiting. They released Revere and headed back to their command, taking Revere's horse with them.

His heroics didn't end here though, because he spent the rest of the day getting the house of Reverend Jonas Clarke's to meet with John Hancock and to assist him and his family to escape from the town.

This is something that few people know about Paul Revere - he served as a messenger during his famous midnight ride, but he also worked as a messenger during the actual Battles of Lexington and Concord.

The Result of the Ride

Something that everyone needs to know about the "midnight ride of Paul Revere" is that it really did happen and that it proved to the colonists that their militia system would work. They had used their "alarm" and "muster" system during the hours leading to the battle, and it worked beautifully.

For example, it is said that "this system was so effective that people in towns 25 miles from Boston were aware of the army's movements while they were still unloading boats in Cambridge". This was without radios, cell phones, or any other form of communication except men riding on horses!

Of course, many people point out that Paul Revere's military life had already prepared him for his mad dash to Concord. This was because he had served as a messenger of sorts during his time in the French Indian War and because he was an active member of the "Committee of Public Safety" in Boston. His job on the Committee was to deliver messages about any political trouble in New York City to delegates and groups in Philadelphia. Clearly, he was a master in the saddle and also knew how to ride without being captured - even in hostile or dangerous areas.

So, you now know that the story of the midnight ride is mostly true. It is unfortunate that the ride is often the only heroic deed that Paul Revere is given credit for because he actually showed great courage leading up to the declaration of the war against Britain and many times afterward. His great mind was also of tremendous use in making ammunitions and more.

What is so interesting about the poem that has created all of the legend around Revere is the simple fact that the author, Henry Wadsworth Longfellow, admits that he bent the truth a bit in order to establish Revere as a true icon and legendary figure. He did accomplish this goal, but many historians and scholars have worked hard to show that the "real" Paul Revere is even more fascinating than the mythical one from the poem.

This is best seen when you look at his military career during the war.

Chapter 6: Paul Revere's Military Career

Let's look at Paul Revere's military career by first considering what it would have been like to be a soldier during that war. For one thing you would have walked everywhere. Very few soldiers had the luxury of a "mount" and wagons were not a typical military transport.

You would have been given only a few items by the government, and sometimes there might not have been enough of these items to go around. If you were fortunate you received:

- A "cocked hat" with three corners and which was made of felt (a wool fabric)

- A heavy linen shirt

- A vest or "weskit"

- One pair of handmade wool socks

- "Common" shoes that were made to be worn on either foot (so you would have very uncomfortable shoes indeed)

- One pair of pants or breeches

- A regimental coat made of heavy wool and in the color of your regiment or group

- A flintlock musket

- A bayonet

- A box for ammunition

- A canteen for water

- A sack to carry all of your food

- A knapsack meant to carry personal items apart from gear and food

Soldiers were often given their food to carry or were fed by a camp cook each day. The food was very limited. Most soldiers were lucky if they were able to eat:

- One pound of meat

- A measure of dried beans

- A measure of rum

- One pound of bread

Most soldiers were given less than half of this amount each day!

The lack of food must have been extremely tiring because if soldiers were not fighting in battle, they were usually doing "drills" to prepare for battle. Everything was done by the sound of a drum, and this is why there are still "fife and drum corps" playing Revolutionary era music!

Paul Revere's Life

Was this the sort of military life that Paul Revere had? No, and that was not because he was privileged but also because he was not immediately allowed into the army!

Following the Battles of Lexington and Concord he could not return home to Boston. His family was able to eventually get out of the city to meet him, and the Continental Congress asked him to help them with an ammunition problem. There were no mills available to make gunpowder, and so Revere was asked to head to Philadelphia to learn about the workings of a powder mill. He succeeded in his quest and was able to create the incredibly useful and successful Stoughton powder mill that made tons of gunpowder for the colonial militia.

By 1776, he was finally allowed to enter into the Massachusetts militia as a major in the infantry. This is when his military service would begin to look like a typical soldier's. He was "on the road" for many years after that traveling from Castle William in Boston harbor to Vermont in order to fight in the Battle of Bennington. He was also sent to the states of Rhode Island and Maine during the war.

He was not able to match the glory of that midnight ride, and some might say that his military life ended with a bit of a fizzle. This is because he was involved in what came to be known as the "Penobscot Expedition", or what some called a disaster.

What happened was that Revere and his fellow militiamen were sent to eliminate the British lodging in Penobscot Bay in Maine. There was a huge clash in the "chain of command" and the commanders on land would not agree with the commanders on shore.

There are many questions about what happened during the mission, but in short the two groups could not agree on the best approach and a siege rather than a direct attack was ordered (this meant that the militia would sit and fire cannons and weaponry from a distance rather than charging in and taking over). Revere was against the siege, but eventually agreed with the naval commander to return with troops to the ships.

The next day the ships came under attack from some British ships, and the entire militia fleet tried to retreat up the Penobscot River. The artillery group, with Revere in command, was put ashore and their ships were then destroyed. A Brigadier General had ordered Revere to send his transport into the river to attempt to get a boat that had gotten away from the militia, and though Revere first refused, he then went and recovered the boat.

This action, however, separated him from all of the men under his orders. He had to move on land and he had to work hard to gather all of his troops together so they could make their way back to Boston. He was formally charged with all kinds of crimes and even asked to resign his position in the militia in 1779. He fought for many years afterward to clear his name, which did happen in 1782.

It is easy to understand why Revere would be happy to end his years as a soldier and return to life in Boston. He was able to do so when the war came to an end in 1783, and by 1788 he had restored his shop in the North End neighborhood of Boston that had long been his home.

Now, however, he would no longer work silver since there was really no market for the precious metal. First he opened a home goods and hardware store, and then shifted back into metal working, with an emphasis on brass. You see, Paul Revere's later life would be filled with the sound of bells!

Chapter 7: Later Life

*Paul Revere late in life painted
by Gilbert Stuart*

What did life have in store for Paul Revere in the years after the Revolutionary War? Well, he established himself as a leading maker of church bells. There was a religious era in the country known as the "Second Great Awakening" and many churches were constructed.

Revere got into the metal casting business and worked with his son, Paul Jr. to create "Paul Revere & Sons" and to make more than 900 bells during his lifetime. In fact, Revere's company made the very first cast bell in Boston!

They also had a lot of business that came from making heavy duty metal parts for the shipbuilding industry that was now thriving in Boston.

By the turn of the century, in 1801, he was also beginning to use copper to a tremendous degree. He opened the nation's very first copper mill in Canton, Massachusetts and produced the copper sheets that appeared on the dome of the State House as well.

This shows us that he was still a forward thinker because he was able to convert metal working from what had always been viewed as a "cottage industry" to a very large and prosperous commercial venture. He never abandoned the craftsman idea behind metal work, but he was able to take the idea and expand it into a very major industry!

THE

FEDERALIST:

A COLLECTION OF

E S S A Y S,

WRITTEN IN FAVOUR OF THE

NEW CONSTITUTION,

AS AGREED-UPON BY THE

FEDERAL CONVENTION,

SEPTEMBER 17, 1787.

Revere as Federalist

This can be seen even more clearly when, in the 1780s, he came out as a big supporter for Secretary of the Treasury Alexander Hamilton's policies for industrialization and a strong central bank. This means that Revere was one of the first "Federalists," as well as one of the Sons of Liberty and a patriot.

The Federalists were the very first American political party and their goal was to create a very strong and "nationalistic" government. This meant that they wanted a "national bank" and good trade relations with other large countries that were helped by tariffs, or beneficial taxes.

How would that support the growth of the nation? It helps to know about the other model that was put in place by Thomas Jefferson. He wanted a decentralized government. He meant that government should not actually play a part in the day to day lives of citizens but instead serve as a sort of outline and guiding set of laws and principles. Jefferson envisioned an "agrarian" or farming and small community model that did not include anything more than cottage industries. While we can never know if his model would have worked, we can see that his vision did not quite fit with others of his era.

The strength of the Federalist idea for big business was proven by the success of Revere's companies and business enterprises. He eventually created the enormous and nation-wide business known as Revere Copper and Brass, which is a company that was taken over by his son, Joseph Warren Revere, when he died and which still operates today!

He firmly believed that industrialization was the key to a strong economy and an even stronger country. He was able to see business almost everywhere he set his eye, which is proven by his successes before, during and after the war. For instance, he began selling home goods and hardware as soon as the country started to recover from the war - at a time when people were in desperate need of everything from sewing needles to wash boards.

He also recognized the market for church bells long before anyone else, and went ahead and studied the art of casting metal into bells in order to be ready to meet the demand for such unique items. He also knew that his machinery would be able to create the shipbuilding supplies that would soon be in demand in Boston. Before he was 65 he had done just about everything a single person might achieve, and even more!

It is interesting to note that Paul Revere saw the very beginning of the United States, played a huge role in making it happen, suffered a bit of failure during his time in the military and yet emerged as a successful business professional. He was always an active person, and kept an interest in the things that went on in the American government. He remained a dedicated resident of Boston, and even offered his services in protecting the city during the War of 1812.

Today it is often forgotten that he created a massive company that is still thriving, even with all of the wars and economic troubles that the country has experienced since the 1770s. Many don't realize that he was an artist with silver and metal and that many museums still display some of his creations as works of art rather than purely historic items. Many also don't recall that he was a master engraver who created many excellent scenes and images that captured moments leading up to the Revolutionary War, and even events that happened during the war.

Because he made so many church bells it is possible that most of the people in New England have heard at least one bell that was created in his workshop as well!

It is very easy to see that Paul Revere was a person with a lot of vision and skills. He challenged authority from an early age, but also showed that he was a very logical and reasonable person. From his early exploration of different religions to his fighting the tyranny of British rule, and even to his idea of "one if by land, two if by sea" as a way to communicate the threat of attack, he was truly one of America's first innovators.

He died at the age of 83 in 1818 - many years before the famous poem about him was written or published. In fact, Paul Revere was not a Revolutionary War hero when he died. He was not even remembered as a great patriot. It was his commitment to charity and business that people spoke of after his death, but today we can finally see him for the great American hero that he truly is!

Conclusion

American history has a lot of different heroes, but one very unusual hero is Paul Revere. Most people know him from the poem that talks about his famous ride to warn the militia, patriots, and citizens of the approach of the British "regulars". We understand today that the poem is a bit of an exaggeration, but we also know that it is almost impossible to exaggerate the life of Paul Revere after that famous ride.

What he accomplished in his lifetime was absolutely amazing. He went from being the son of an immigrant silversmith to one of the country's greatest patriots. He fought bravely through the war and gave freely of his time and energy. After the war he helped to nurture and build the economy of the nation, and he remained a tremendously active member of his community right up to the end of his life.

We should remember that famous midnight ride, but we should also remember that Paul Revere was able to accomplish much more than one heroic act in his lifetime, and that it is just as important to know him for his other contributions to history as well.

He is buried in the Old Granary Burying Ground on Tremont Street, Boston and many people visit his marker. We hope you have enjoyed learning the true story of Paul Revere!

Web Resources

1. bio.Classroom - Bio4Kids: Paul Revere is a great guide to the life and times of Paul Revere and gives good information about his life before and after the war. See the site at:
    http://www.biography.com/assets/pdf/study_guides/bio4kids/Bio4KidsPaulRevere.pdf

2. The History Place - The English Colonial Era pages tell a lot more about America before the Revolution. This is a fun and easy to read timeline that takes you through all of the years from 1700 to 1763. See the facts at:
    http://www.historyplace.com/unitedstates/revolution/rev-col.htm

3. Kid's History of the American Revolution: this website is packed with all kinds of interesting material that explains everything you need to know about the Revolutionary War. Visit the site at:

http://www.kidport.com/reflib/usahist
ory/AmericanRevolution/AmerRevoluti
on.htm

4. Liberty's Kids: the Paul Revere page on
   this site is only the tip of the iceberg. If
   you want to know about Revere and his
   era, this is the site. See it here at:
   http://libertyskids.com/arch_who_preve
   re.html

5. The Paul Revere Heritage Project: an
   amazing website packed with details and
   facts. From myths to documents, you will
   find everything Revere at:
   http://www.paul-revere-
   heritage.com/biography/later-years.html

6. "Paul Revere's Ride" - use this link to
   read the entire poem about the famous
   "midnight ride of Paul Revere" as written
   by Henry Wadsworth Longfellow. Find
   the site at:
   http://poetry.eserver.org/paul-
   revere.html

7. Places to See Paul Revere's work - use this
   link to see a list of the online and real

world galleries where you can go and see the works made by Paul Revere and his silversmith shop. See the details at: http://www.artcyclopedia.com/artists/r evere_paul.html

8. Revere Speaks: want to hear the words from Revere himself? This site gives his explanation of the famous midnight ride! See it all at: http://www.americanrevolution.org/rev ere.html

9. Soldier in the Revolutionary War: read what it was really like to be a soldier during the war and understand just how challenging it was. Visit: http://www.vancortlandthouse.org/Sold ier%20in%20the%20Revolutionary%20Wa r.htm

10. Ten Facts about Paul Revere: interested in knowing everything possible about Paul Revere? Read these facts to discover some little known details by visiting: http://www.surfnetkids.com/go/64/ten -facts-about-paul-revere/

Made in the USA
Coppell, TX
26 January 2021

48885801R00039